Mack Wilberg
Anthems

9 anthems for mixed voices
by Mack Wilberg

MUSIC DEPARTMENT

OXFORD
UNIVERSITY PRESS

OXFORD

UNIVERSITY PRESS

Great Clarendon Street, Oxford OX2 6DP,
United Kingdom

Oxford University Press is a department of the University of Oxford.
It furthers the University's objective of excellence in research, scholarship,
and education by publishing worldwide. Oxford is a registered trade mark of
Oxford University Press in the UK and in certain other countries

First published 2013

Impression: 4

ISBN 978-0-19-339819-1

Music and text origination by
Enigma Music Production Services, Amersham Bucks.

Printed in Great Britain on acid-free paper by
Halstan & Co. Ltd, Amersham, Bucks.

Contents

Composer's note

Most of the music in this collection was written for choirs I have had the privilege of working with over the past thirty years. Included are both original works and arrangements, as well as two commissioned pieces published here for the first time.

I have made new SATB versions of several pieces originally written for men's voices and also reduced the accompaniment from piano, four-hands to organ only for one of the arrangements. With the exception of the unaccompanied pieces, all selections included in the collection may be sung with alternative orchestral accompaniment (see page 4 for details).

I would like to thank David Blackwell for his invaluable assistance in the making of this volume.

MACK WILBERG
June 2013

Index of Orchestrations and Vocal Scores

The following items are also available as listed below:
- Scores and orchestral parts on hire/rental from the publisher or appropriate agent;
- Separate vocal scores on sale.

Benediction
- Orchestration: 2fl, ob, 2cl, 4hn, harp, strings
- Vocal score for SATB and keyboard (piano or organ) on sale: 978-0-19-337223-8

Brother James's Air
- Orchestration: 2fl, 2ob, 2cl, 2bsn, 4hn, strings
- Vocal score for SATB and keyboard (piano or organ) on sale: 978-0-19-337224-5

I sing the mighty power of God
- Orchestration: picc, fl, ob, 3hn, perc, glock, harp (opt.), strings
- Vocal score for SATB and organ on sale: 978-0-19-386923-3

King of glory, King of peace
- Orchestration: 2fl, picc/fl3, 2ob, 2cl, 2bsn, 2hn, 2tpt, timp, perc, glock, harp, strings

Morning has broken
- Orchestration: 3fl, 2ob, 2cl, 2bsn, 4hn, glock, harp, strings
- Vocal score for SATB and piano four-hands on sale: 978-0-19-380463-0

O Light of Life!
- Orchestration: 3fl, 2ob, 2cl, 2bsn, 4hn, organ (opt.), strings
- Vocal score for SATB and organ (3 staves) on sale: 978-0-19-380459-3

O little town of Bethlehem
- Orchestration: picc, fl, ob, 3hn, perc (glock), harp (opt.), strings

O praise ye the Lord
- Orchestration: 3fl, 2ob, 2cl, 2bsn, 4hn, 3tpt, 3tbne, tba, timp, perc, organ, strings

The Morning Trumpet
- Vocal score for unaccompanied lower voices (TTBB) on sale: 978-0-19-386828-1

Available Recordings

Beautiful Saviour
The version for men's voices has been recorded on the CD *Men of the Mormon Tabernacle Choir* (SKU 5053126).

Benediction
The orchestral arrangement has been recorded by the Mormon Tabernacle Choir and the Orchestra at Temple Square on the CD *Heavensong: Music of Contemplation and Light* (SKU 5035926).

Brother James's Air
The orchestral arrangement has been recorded by the Mormon Tabernacle Choir and the Orchestra at Temple Square on the CD *Heavensong: Music of Contemplation and Light* (SKU 5035926).

I sing the mighty power of God
The orchestral arrangement has been recorded by the Mormon Tabernacle Choir and the Orchestra at Temple Square on the CD *Consider the Lilies* (SKU 4537795).

Morning has broken
The orchestral arrangement has been recorded by the Mormon Tabernacle Choir and the Orchestra at Temple Square on the CD *Consider the Lilies* (SKU 4537795).

O Light of Life!
The orchestral arrangement has been recorded by the Mormon Tabernacle Choir and the Orchestra at Temple Square on the CD *Mack Wilberg: Requiem and other choral works* (SKU 4996466).

The Morning Trumpet
The version for men's voices has been recorded on the CD *Men of the Mormon Tabernacle Choir* (SKU 5053126).

originally written for the Brigham Young University Men's Chorus

Beautiful Saviour

Anon., 12th century

Silesian Folk Melody
arr. MACK WILBERG

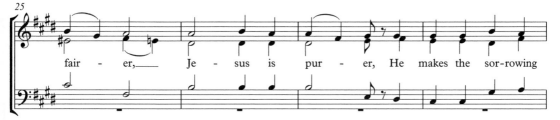

fair - er,___ Je - sus is pur - er, He makes the sor-rowing

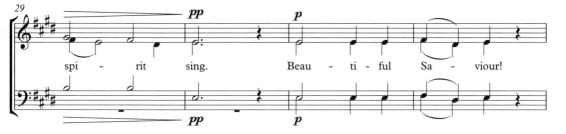

spi - rit sing.   Beau - ti - ful Sa - viour!

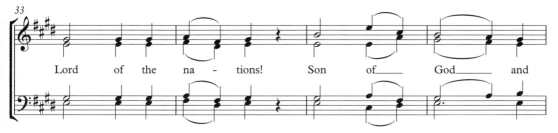

Lord   of   the   na - tions!   Son   of___   God___   and

Son___   of   Man!___   Thee   will   I   hon - our,___

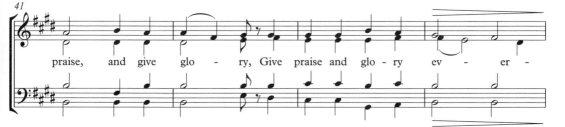

praise,   and   give   glo - ry,   Give   praise and   glo - ry   ev - er -

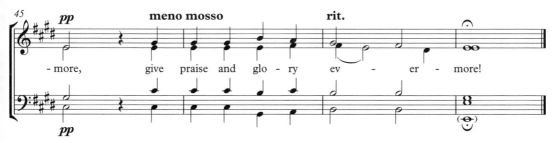

- more,   give   praise   and   glo - ry   ev - er - more!

for the Mormon Tabernacle Choir and Orchestra at Temple Square

Benediction

David Warner

MACK WILBERG

*The keyboard part may be played on piano or organ and adapted as necessary.

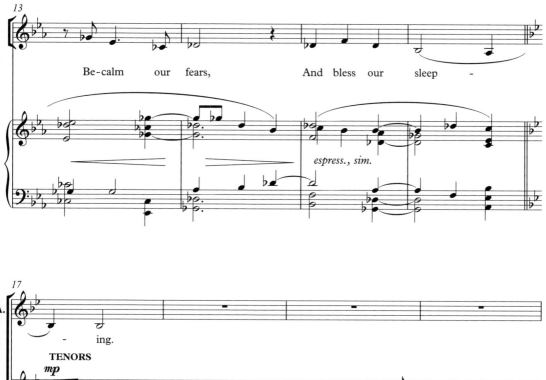

Be-calm our fears, And bless our sleep -

- ing.

TENORS
mp

Come to us this day, A-wake our hearts,

Re-new our minds, And bless our ris - -

Come to us, we pray, Re-ceive our love,

- ing. Come,— we pray,_____ Re - ceive our

Come to us, we pray,_____ Re-ceive our

- ing. Come, we pray,_____ Re - ceive our

Be-hold our joy, And bless our prais - -

love,_____ Be - hold our joy,___ our prais - -

love,_____ Be-hold our joy,___ our prais - -

love,_____ Be - hold our joy,___ our prais - -

for the Mormon Tabernacle Choir and Orchestra at Temple Square

Brother James's Air

JAMES LEITH MACBETH BAIN (*c.*1840–1925)
arr. MACK WILBERG

Psalm 23 (adap.)

*The keyboard part may be played on piano or organ and adapted as necessary.

for the Mormon Tabernacle Choir and Orchestra at Temple Square

I sing the mighty power of God
O little town of Bethlehem

Isaac Watts (1674–1748), altd
Phillips Brooks (1835–95)

Trad. English
arr. MACK WILBERG

I 8', 4', 1⅓'
II 8'
Pedal 16', 8'

This piece may be sung using either set of lyrics.

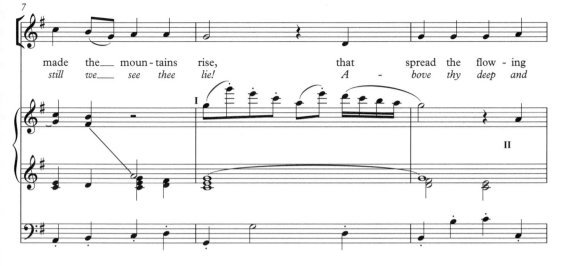

made the— moun-tains rise,   that   spread the flow - ing
still   we— see   thee   lie!   *A - bove   thy   deep   and*

seas_   a - broad and built the— loft - y skies.   I—
dream - less— sleep The   si - lent— stars   go   by.   *Yet—*

sing   the wis - dom— that— or - dained the sun to rule the
in   thy dark— streets_ shin - eth The   ev - er - last - ing

*When using the alternative text (O little town of Bethlehem), this note should be held for a crotchet/quarter note.

44

flow'r   be - low   but   makes   thy___   glo - ries   known;   and
Beth - le - hem,   De - scend   to___   us,   we   pray;   Cast

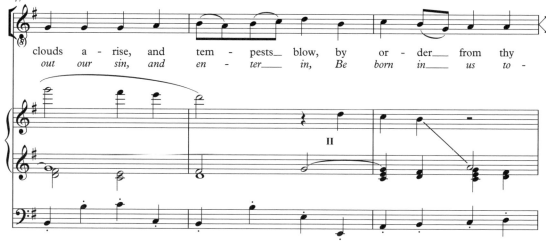

47

clouds   a - rise,   and   tem - pests__   blow,   by   or - der__   from   thy
out   our   sin,   and   en - ter__   in,   Be   born   in__   us   to -

II

50

S.
A.

throne;   while__   all__   that   bor - rows   life__   from_   thee   is
- day.   We__   hear__   the   Christ - mas__   an   -   gels   The

(T. & B. *unis.*)

B.

I

62   slightly slower

ev - 'ry - where that   we___ can___ be,_____   thou,
come   to   us,   a -   bide___ with___ us,_____   Our

mp

65   rit.   tempo I

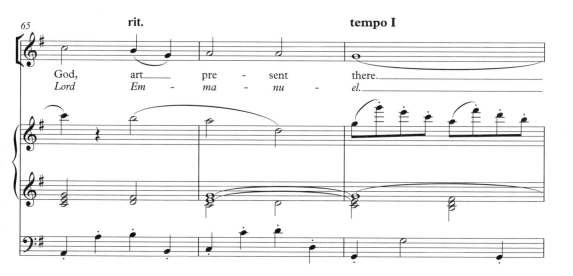

God,   art___ pre - sent there._____
Lord   Em - ma - nu - el._____

68

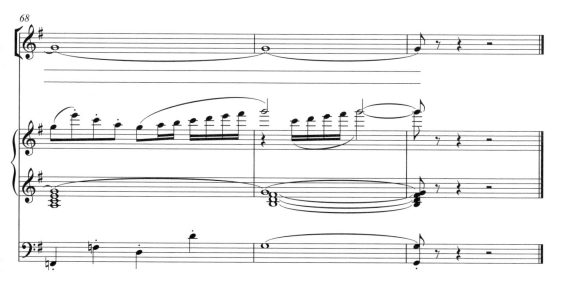

*Commissioned by Dr Frederic G. Sanford, II,
for the Harrisburg Singers, Harrisburg, PA. (Susan Beckley, conductor) and the American Composers' Choral Festival
and in loving memory of Mary Jane Sharpless Sanford*

King of glory, King of peace

George Herbert (1593–1633)

MACK WILBERG

and,_ that love may nev - er cease,_ I_ will move_ thee._

T./B. Thou hast grant-ed my_ re-quest, thou_ hast heard me;

thou didst note my work - ing breast,

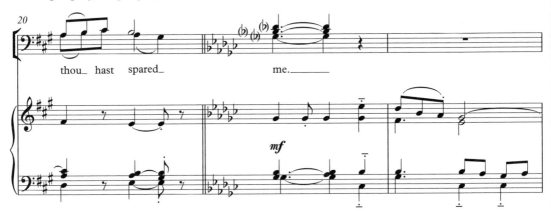

thou_ hast   spared_   me._____

S.
A.

Where-fore with my   ut - most art____   I__ will sing__   thee,

T.
B.

and__   the cream of   all__   my heart   I____   will bring__

thee._____

S./A. *unis.* **mp**
Though my sins a - gainst me cried,

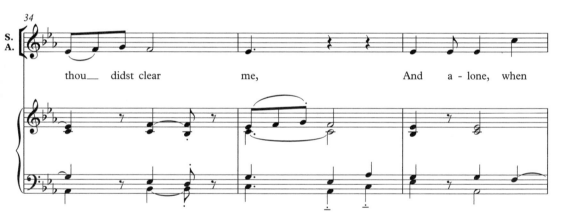

thou__ didst clear   me,   And   a - lone, when

they__ re - plied,   thou__ didst hear   me._____

Sev'n_ whole days, not   one_   in   sev'n,_

I_ will praise_ thee;   in_ my heart, though not_ in heav'n,

I_ can raise_   thee._

Small it is, in this_ poor sort,_ to_ en - rol_ thee;

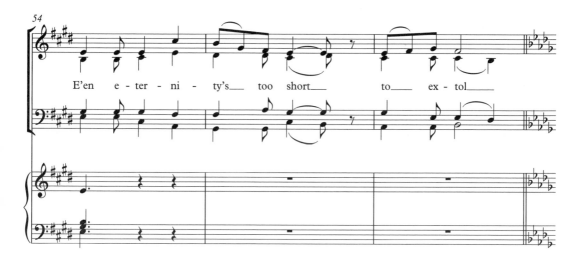

E'en e - ter - ni - ty's_ too short_ to_ ex - tol_

thee,_   to   thee,_   to

- ty's_ too short to_____ ex - tol_____ thee,

to   thee,_____   to   thee._____

for the Mormon Tabernacle Choir and Orchestra at Temple Square

Morning has broken

Eleanor Farjeon (1881–1965)

Trad. Gaelic melody
arr. MACK WILBERG

Also available in a version for SATB and piano four-hands (ISBN 978-0-19-380463-0). Both this version and the orchestral accompaniment (see p. 4) have a more extended introduction to verses 1 and 2.

sing - ing,   praise for the morn - ing,   praise for them,
sweet - ness   of the wet gar - den,   spung in com -

spring - ing   fresh from the Word!
- plete - ness   where his feet   pass.

3. Mine is the sun – light; mine is the morn – ing,_____ born of the

one light E-den saw play!_____ Praise with e - la – tion, praise ev-'ry

morn - ing God's re-cre - a - tion of the new day!

dim.

SOPRANOS & ALTOS
unis. **mp**

Praise with e - la - tion, praise ev - 'ry

mp

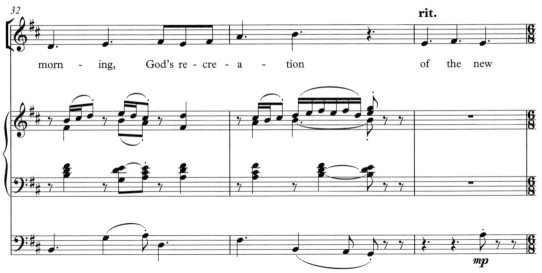

morn - ing,   God's re - cre - a - tion   of   the   new

day!

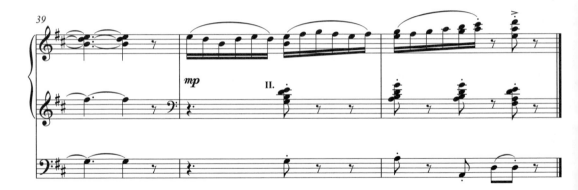

O Light of Life!

David Warner

MACK WILBERG

O Light of Life! O pure Light Di - vine! Thou art in us; Our em - ber is Thine. Kin - dle our faith, Give

hope when we fear, Deep - en our love— Thy Fire___ ap-

- pear! Light of our souls, Thou spark at our birth—

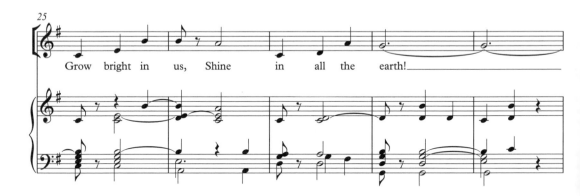

Grow bright in us, Shine in all the earth!_____

TENORS & BASSES
unis. **mf**

_____ O Light of Life! O true Light of

Peace! Storms will a - rise, Let Thy light in - crease.

Pierce through dark clouds, Give pause to the proud; Let Thy shafts

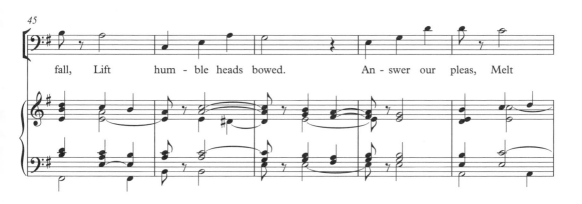

fall, Lift hum - ble heads bowed. An - swer our pleas, Melt

hearts in Thy flame. Make us as one— As one in Thy

- pace._____ See the bright Tree! Be - hold the white
*(On through the night, Walk with us we

fruit!_____ Feast - ing we weep, We wit - ness the root!
pray._____ Lead us to dawn, Thy mer - ci - ful way.)

Exultantly

O Light of Life! O dear Light of Love! Come, wash us

*Alternative lyrics.

clean, Send forth Thy white Dove. Fill us with

Fire, En - light - en our eyes;___ Help us to love— 'Tis

price of the prize.___ Then let us come, En - robe us in

white._____   Cleav - ing   to   Thee, Light   un - to Thy

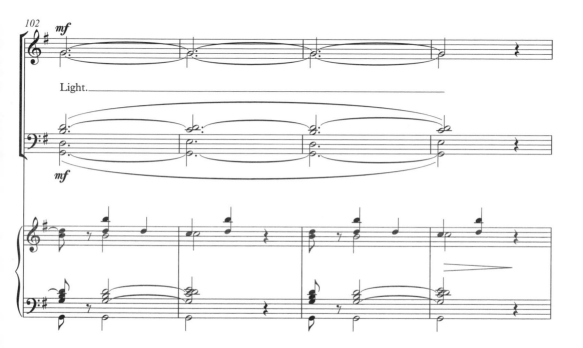

Light._____

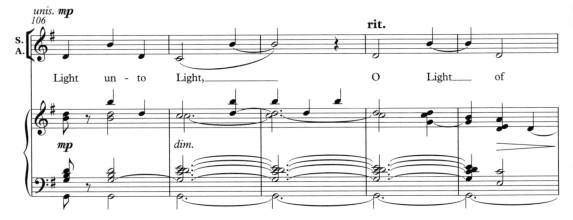

Light   un - to   Light,_____   O   Light____   of

Life!_____

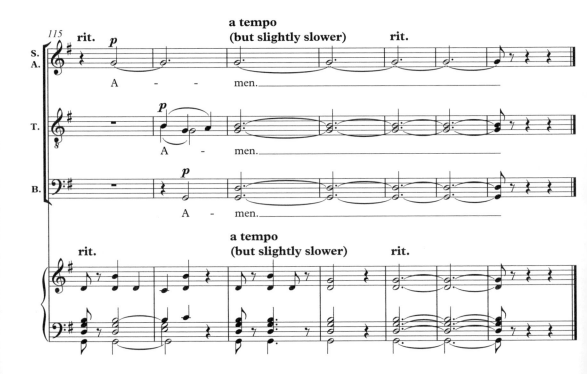

A   -   -   men._____

A   -   men._____

A   -   men._____

Commissioned in loving memory of Jack Richard Harding
for the Sanctuary Choir of Preston Hollow Presbyterian Church, Dallas, Texas; Terry Price, Director

O praise ye the Lord

C. HUBERT H. PARRY (1848–1918)
(Laudate Dominum)
arr. MACK WILBERG

Henry W. Baker (1821–77), alt.

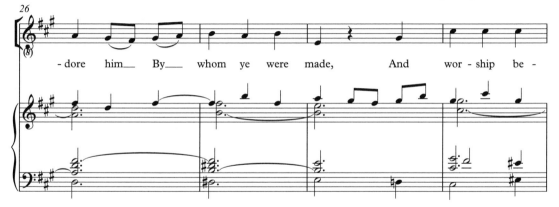

-dore him__ By__ whom ye were made, And wor - ship be -

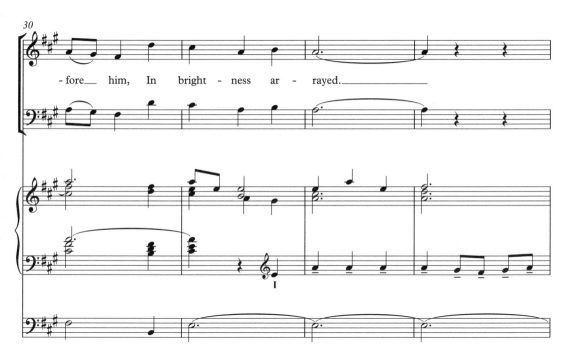

-fore__ him, In bright - ness ar - rayed._____

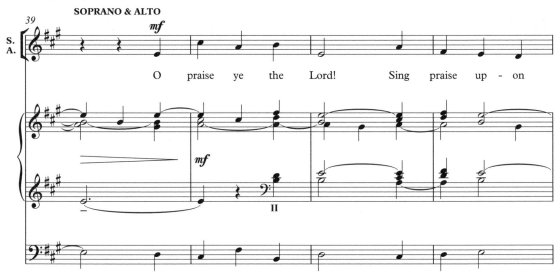

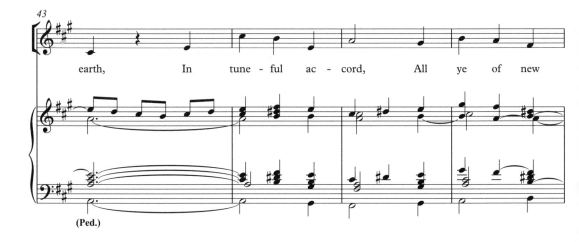

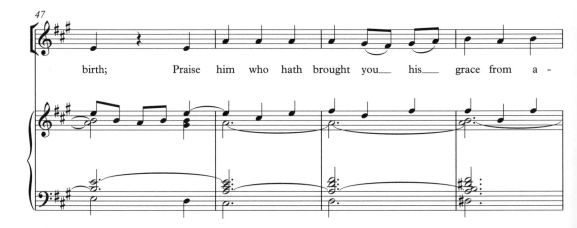

- bove, Praise him who hath taught you to sing of his

love._____

O praise ye the____

Lord!   All   things   that   give   sound;   Each   ju - bi - lant

chord___   re - e - cho   a - round;   Loud   or - gans,   his

glo - ry___   forth___   tell   in   deep   tone,   And   sweet harp,   the

sto - ry   of   what   he   hath   done.

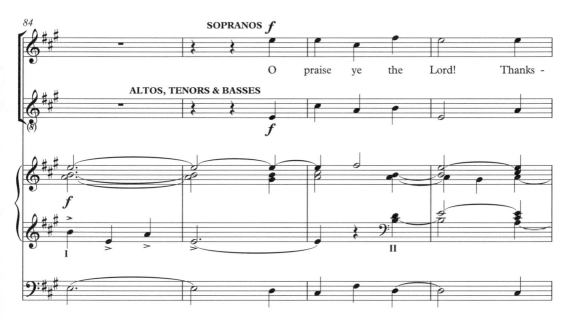

SOPRANOS *f*

O praise ye the Lord! Thanks -

ALTOS, TENORS & BASSES

- gi - ving and song   To   him   be   out - poured_   all

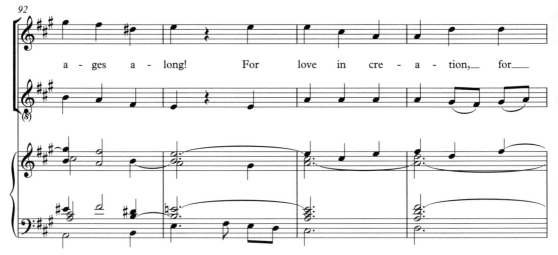

a - ges a - long! For love in cre - a - tion,__ for__

hea - ven re - stored! For grace of sal - va - tion, O

praise ye the Lord!

originally written for Brigham Young University Men's Chorus

The Morning Trumpet

John Leland (1754–1841)

B. F. White (1800–79)*
arr. MACK WILBERG

With marked rhythm and articulation ♩ = 88

SOPRANO
ALTO

TENOR
BASS

T./B. unis.

O when shall I see Je - sus and reign with him a - bove, And shall

S./A.. unis.

And from the flow-ing

hear** the trum-pet sound_ in that morn - ing;

foun - tain drink ev - er - last - ing love, And shall hear the trum - pet

sound in that morn - ing. O___ shout with glo - ry! I shall

*From *The Sacred Harp* (1844).
**The 'h' of 'hear' should be given emphasis throughout.

mount a-bove the skies When I hear the trum-pet sound in that morn -

- ing. O__ shout with glo - ry! I shall mount a-bove the skies When I

hear the trum - pet sound__ in that morn - - ing.

sound, sound the trum - pet, the trum - pet, the

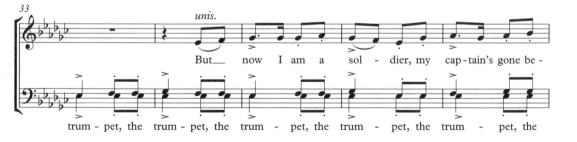

unis.

But__ now I am a sol - dier, my cap-tain's gone be -

trum - pet, the trum - pet, the trum - pet, the trum - pet, the trum - pet, the

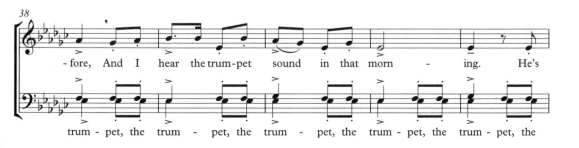

- fore, And I hear the trum-pet sound in that morn - ing. He's

trum - pet, the trum - pet, the trum - pet, the trum - pet, the trum - pet, the

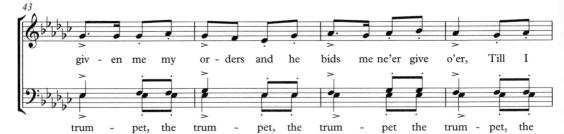

giv - en me my or - ders and he bids me ne'er give o'er, Till I

trum - pet, the trum - pet, the trum - pet the trum - pet, the

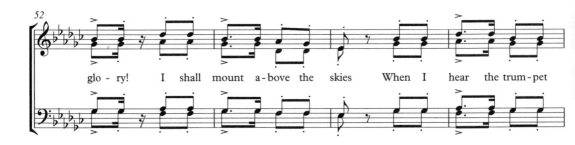

hear the trum-pet sound in that morn - - ing. O___ shout with

trum - pet, the trum - pet, the trum - pet, the trump.

glo - ry! I shall mount a-bove the skies When I hear the trum-pet

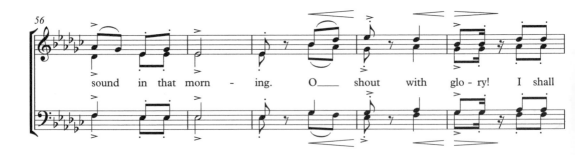

sound in that morn - ing. O___ shout with glo - ry! I shall

mount a-bove the skies When I hear the trum - pet sound_ in that

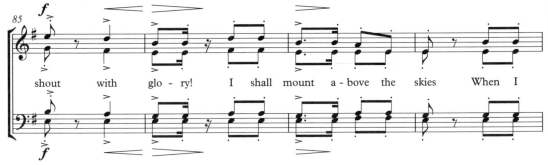

shout with glo - ry! I shall mount a - bove the skies When I

hear the trum - pet sound_ in that morn - ing. O____

shout with glo - ry! I shall mount a - bove the skies When I

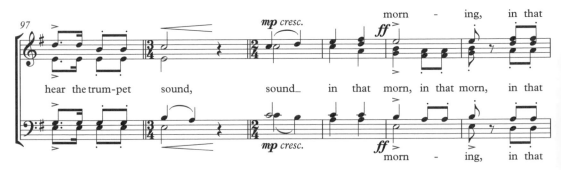

morn - ing, in that

hear the trum-pet sound, sound_ in that morn, in that morn, in that

morn - ing, in that

morn - - ing,

morn, in that morn, in that morn, in that morn, in that morn - ing.

morn - ing,